— LOST RIVER —

ALSO BY JAMES TATE

Dreams of a Robot Dancing Bee (2001)
Memoir of the Hawk (2001)
The Route as Briefed (1999)
Shroud of the Gnome (1997)
Worshipful Company of Fletchers (1995)
Selected Poems (1991)
Distance from Loved Ones (1990)
Reckoner (1986)
Constant Defender (1983)
Riven Doggeries (1980)
Viper Jazz (1976)
Absences (1972)
Hints to Pilgrims (1971)
The Oblivion Ha-Ha (1970)

LOST RIVER

Quarternote Chapbook Series #2

Sarabande Books

Louisville, Kentucky

JAMES TATE

Managing Editor
Sarabande Books, Inc.
2234 Dundee Road, Suite 200
Louisville, KY 40205

LIBRARY OF CONGRESS CATALOGING-IN-PUBLICATION DATA

Tate, James, 1943–
Lost river : poems / by James Tate.
p.   cm.
(Quarternote chapbook series ; #2)
ISBN 1-889330-84-1 (pbk. : alk. paper)
I. Title. II. Series.
PS3570.A8 L67 2003
811'.54—dc21
2002007235/

Cover and text design by Charles Casey Martin.

Manufactured in the United States of America.
This book is printed on acid-free paper.

Sarabande Books is nonprofit literary organization.

Funded in part by a grant from the Kentucky Arts Council, a state agency
of the Education, Arts, and Humanities Cabinet.

Acknowledgments: *Boston Review, Both, The Germ, Harvard Review,
TriQuarterly, Virginia Quarterly Review*

FIRST EDITION

CONTENTS

The Memories of Fish

Stanley took a day off from the office
and spent the whole day talking to fish in
his aquarium. To the little catfish scuttling
along the bottom he said, "Vacuum that scum,
boy. Suck it up, that's your job." The skinny
pencil fish swam by and he said, "Scribble,
scribble, scribble. Write me a novel, needle-
nose." The angel executed a particularly
masterful left-turn and Stanley said, "You're
no angel, but you sure can drive." Then he broke
for lunch and made himself a tuna fish sandwich
the irony of which did not escape him. Oh no,
he wallowed in it, savoring every bite. Then
he returned to his chair in front of the aquarium.
A swarm of tiny neons amused him. "What do you
think this is, Times Square!" he shouted. And
so it went long into the night. The next morning
Stanley was horribly embarrassed by his behavior
and he apologized to the fish several times,
but they never really forgave him. He had mocked
their very fishiness, and for this there can be
no forgiveness.

The All but Perfect Evening on the Lake

We were at the lake for the weekend. We
had just come back from canoeing. We had seen
the loons and a couple of deer and an eagle.
Cleo was taking a shower and I had just opened
a bottle of wine. There was a fire going in
the fireplace. I had worked hard for all of
this, but still I felt like the luckiest man
on earth. When Cleo finally joined me I knew
it was true. She was stunning. "It was a great
day, honey," she said, "thank you." "You're
what makes it great for me, and I can't thank
you enough," I said. I poured us some wine and
we stared at the fire. About an hour later,
there was a knock at the door. This in itself
was a little disconcerting because there are so
few people around here. I looked at Cleo and
she shrugged her shoulders and grimaced. I
opened the door and there was a ranger standing
there. "Are you Eric and Cleo Martin?" he asked.
"Yes, sir," I said. "What seems to be the
problem?" "You're under arrest," he said.
"What in the world for?" I asked, utterly
confused. "Too much happiness," he said.
"The folks around here have registered several
complaints, and there are laws that limit this
kind of thing on the lake. You'll both have
to come with me." "Is this some kind of joke?"
I asked. "I'll have to look in my book," he
said. And then he pulled a thick leather

book out of his coat and carefully turned the
pages until he found the appropriate entry.
He studied it for a minute or so, running
his finger down the page. Finally
he said, "Yes, definitely, this is some kind of
joke, but I'm unable to determine which
kind. Is that okay, would that bother you
if I can't tell you what kind of joke it is?"
I looked at Cleo. "We don't care. Well,
goodnight, officer. Have a good evening."
"And you folks go right back to being happy,"
he said. "Goodnight."

Never Enough Darts

A bear walked right into town last week.
It was a big one, too, a male. It pushed open
the door of the pizza place and ate all the
pizza off the customers' plates. People just
sat there with their mouths open, impressed.
Then he just walked on down the street and went
in the hamburger joint and did the same thing.
The cook managed to call the police. The police
came right away, but they had used up all of
their knock-out darts at last Friday night's
high school football game. So they just followed
the bear at a polite distance. When the bear
was full it found its way out of town. The
people I talked to seemed delighted to be getting
back to nature. As long as they had enough to
eat they weren't going to complain.

Making the Best of the Holidays

Justine called on Christmas day to say she was thinking of killing herself. I said, "We're in the middle of opening presents, Justine. Could you possibly call back later, that is, if you're still alive." She was furious with me and called me all sorts of names which I refuse to dignify by repeating them. I hung up on her and returned to the joyful task of opening presents. Everyone seemed delighted with what they got, and that definitely includes me. I placed a few more logs on the fire, and then the phone rang again. This time it was Hugh and he had just taken all of his pills and washed them down with a quart of gin. "Sleep it off, Hugh," I said, "I can barely under-stand you, you're slurring so badly. Call me tomorrow, Hugh, and Merry Christmas." The roast in the oven smelled delicious. The kids were playing with their new toys. Loni was giving me a big Christmas kiss when the phone rang again. It was Debbie. "I hate you," she said. "You're the most disgusting human being on the planet." "You're absolutely right," I said, "and I've always been aware of this. Nonetheless, Merry Christmas, Debbie." Halfway through dinner the phone rang again, but this time Loni answered it. When she came back to the table she looked pale. "Who was it?" I asked. "It was my mother," she said. "And what did she say?" I asked. "She said she wasn't my mother," she said.

The Florist

       I realized Mother's Day was just two days
away, so I went into the florist and said, "I'd
like to send my mother a dozen long-stem red
roses." The guy looked at me and said, "My mother's
dead." I thought this was slightly unprofessional
of him, so I said, "How much would that be?" He
wiped his eyes and said, "Oh, that's all right. I'm
over it, really. She never loved me anyway, so why
should I grieve." "Can they be delivered by Thursday?"
I inquired. "She hated flowers," he said. "I've
never known a woman to hate flowers the way she did.
She wanted me to be a dentist, like her father.
Can you imagine that, torturing people all day.
Instead, I give them pleasure. She disowned me,
really. And yet I miss her," and then he started
crying again. I gave him my handkerchief and he
blew his nose heartily into it. My annoyance had
given away to genuine pity. This guy was a mess.
I didn't know what to do. Finally I said, "Listen,
why don't you send a dozen roses to my mother. You
can tell her you are a friend of mine. My mother
loves flowers, and she'll love you for sending them
to her." He stopped crying and scowled at me. "Is
this some kind of trick? A trap or something, to
get me tied up in a whole other mother thing, because
if it is, I mean, I just got rid of one, and I can't
take it, another I mean, I'm not as strong as I
appear...." "Forget it," I said, "it was a bad idea,
and I'm certainly not sending my mother any flowers
this year, that too was a bad idea. Will you be

all right if I leave now, I have other errands, but
if you need me I can stay." "Yes, if you could stay
with me awhile. My name is Skeeter and Mother's
Day is always such a trial for me. I miss her more
every passing day," he said. And so we sat there
holding hands for an hour or so, and then I was on
my way to the cleaners, the bank, and the gas station.

Lost River

Jill and I had been driving for hours
on these little back country roads and we hadn't
seen another car or a store of any kind in all
that time. We were trying to get to a village
called Lost River and we were running out of gas.
There was a man there that owns a pterodactyl
wing and we heard that he might want to sell it.
He was tired of it, we were told. Finally, I see
an old pickup truck coming up behind us and I
pull over and get out of the car and wave. The
man starts to pass us by, but changes his mind
and stops. I ask him if he knows how to get to Lost
River and he says he's never heard of it, but
can give us directions to the closest town called
Last Grocery Store. I thank him and we eventually
find Last Grocery Store, which consists of three
trailers and a little bitsy grocery store. The
owner is old and nearly blind, but he's glad to
meet us and we're glad to meet him. I ask him
if he knows how to get to Lost River from here.
He ponders for a while, and then says, "I don't
see how you could get there, unless you're walking.
There's no road out in them parts. Why would
anybody be wanting to go to Lost River, there's
nothing there." "There's a man there that's got
a pterodactyl wing he might be willing to sell,"
I say. "Hell, I'll sell you mine. I can't see
it anymore, so I might as well sell it," he says.
Jill and I look at each other, incredulous. "Well,
we'd sure like to see it," I say. "No problem,"

he says, "I keep it right here in back of the store."
He brings it out and it's beautiful, delicate
and it's real, I'm certain of it. The foot even
has its claws on it. We're speechless and rather
terrified of holding it, though he hands it to us
trustingly. My whole body feels like it's vibrating,
like I'm a harp of time. I'm sort of embarrassed,
but finally I ask him how much he wants for it.
"Oh, just take it. It always brought me luck, but
I've had all the luck I need," he says. Jill gives
him a kiss on the cheek and I shake his hand and
thank him. Tomorrow: Lost River.

Their Number Became Thinned

Judd wrecked his car driving home from
my place the other night. He hit a patch of
black ice and the car spun around out of control
and crashed into a tree. Luckily he wasn't hurt,
and the police report didn't charge him with
anything. When he was telling me about it the
next morning, he went silent for a moment, and
then he said, "I think I hit three little children."
I was shocked because Judd is, for the most part,
a really sane man. "But, Judd," I said, "the
police were there, they filed a report. Trust me,
you didn't hit anyone." "When the car was spinning,"
he said, "I caught the flesh of their faces in
the headlights. There was terror in their eyes.
They looked right at me. I saw them, honest, I
did." "I guess this kind of thing is understand-
able," I said, "given the panic and fear you felt,
but, really, Judd, you didn't hit any children."
I attributed this irrational state of mind to
shock, and assumed it would pass quickly. But
it didn't. In a manner of weeks he began referring
to the kids by name—Tess, Marla, and Cliff. And
I stopped protesting. It's just that he was so
convincing. He would tell me episodes from their
lives. He never mentioned their families. It
was as though they were waifs, playing their
innocent games, biding their time, and always
waiting for Judd's car to hit that black ice.
Eventually, Judd had photographs of them framed,
and when I saw them I recognized them at once.

Lust for Life

Veronica has the best apartment in town.
It's on the third story and has big plate glass
windows that look straight down on the town common.
She has a bird's eye view of all the protesters,
the fairs, the lovers, people eating lunch on
park benches; in general, the life-blood of the
town. The more Veronica watched all these little
dramas, the less desire she had to actually go
out and be one herself. I called her from time
to time, but her conversation consisted of her
descriptions of what was going on in the common.
"Now he's kissing her and saying good-bye. He's
getting on the bus. The bus is pulling out.
Wait a minute, she's just joined hands with
another guy. I can't believe it! These people
are behaving like trash. There's a real tiny
old lady with a walker trying to go into the
bookstore, but she keeps stopping and looking
over her shoulder. She thinks she's being
followed." "Veronica," I say, "I'm dying."
"Two of the richest and nastiest lawyers in
town are arguing over by the drinking fountain.
They're actually shouting, I can almost hear
them. Oh my god, one of them has shoved the
other. It's incredible, Artie. You should be
here," she says. "War has been declared with
England, Veronica. Have you heard that?" I
say. "That's great, Artie," she says. "Remember
the girl who kissed the guy getting on the bus
and then immediately took up with the other guy?

Well, now she's flirting with the parking officer
and he's loving it and flirting back with her.
He just tore up a ticket he had written for her.
I'm really beginning to like this girl after all."
"That's great, Veronica," I say. "Why don't
you check and see if your little panties are
on fire yet," and I hang up, and I don't think
she even notices. I wonder if I'm supposed to
be worried about her. But in the end I don't.
Veronica has the best apartment in town.

It Happens Like This

        I was outside St. Cecilia's Rectory
smoking a cigarette when a goat appeared beside me.
It was mostly black and white, with a little reddish
brown here and there. When I started to walk away,
it followed. I was amused and delighted, but wondered
what the laws were on this kind of thing. There's
a leash law for dogs, but what about goats? People
smiled at me and admired the goat. "It's not my goat,"
I explained. "It's the town's goat. I'm just taking
my turn caring for it." "I didn't know we had a goat,"
one of them said. "I wonder when my turn is." "Soon,"
I said. "Be patient. Your time is coming." The goat
stayed by my side. It stopped when I stopped. It looked
up at me and I stared into its eyes. I felt he knew
everything essential about me. We walked on. A police-
man on his beat looked us over. "That's a mighty
fine goat you got there," he said, stopping to admire it.
"It's the town's goat," I said. "His family goes back
three-hundred years with us," I said, "from the beginning."
The officer leaned forward to touch him, then stopped
and looked up at me. "Mind if I pat him?" he asked.
"Touching this goat will change your life," I said.
"It's your decision." He thought real hard for a minute,
and then stood up and said, "What's his name?" "He's
called the Prince of Peace," I said. "God! This town
is like a fairy tale. Everywhere you turn there's mystery
and wonder. And I'm just a child playing cops and robbers
forever. Please forgive me if I cry." "We forgive you,
Officer," I said. "And we understand why you, more than
anybody, should never touch the Prince." The goat and

19

I walked on. It was getting dark and we were beginning to wonder where we would spend the night.

Cherubic

I took my daughter Kelsey to the train
station. As the train was leaving, we waved
and waved to one another. I never saw her again.
She went on to become the first woman on the moon.
How she got there nobody knew. And she never
came back, as far as I know. And she never wrote
me a letter, she never called. I just hope she's
happy, my moonbeam. Every night I'm at my telescope.
I've seen dinosaurs, snow leopards, flamingos.
I saw a one-eyed dog wagging its tail. I saw a
mail truck. I saw a sailboat, but, of course,
there is no water. I saw a sign for water pointing
to the earth. I saw a sign for hamburgers
pointing to the earth. And I saw a little girl
fall off her tricycle. A poof of atomic tangerine
dust, that's all. I never saw the girl again.
The tumbled tricycle's wheels kept spinning.
Sleep, I said, sleep, little baby.

Being Present at More Than One Place at a Time

I took a step and looked around. No one
was looking, so I took another step. I glanced
at the ground, looked up at the sky. Everything
seemed to be in order, so I took another step,
this one almost a hop. A woman walks up to me
and says, "That was cute." "Thanks," I say,
"watch this," and I leap high into the air.
"That's overdoing things," she says. I hang
my head, ashamed of myself. I stand there for
half-an-hour, not moving, barely breathing.
A cop comes up and says, "You're loitering."
"I'm not loitering," I say, "I'm repositioning
myself. I'm adjusting to the currents."
"My mistake," he says. "You had the appearance
of a loiterer." "It's the fog," I said.
When he was gone, I took a step and looked
around. I could see a vast, golden city on
the horizon. No, it's only the fog, I thought,
and jumped backward, surprising myself.

The Incense Man

Outside the Cigar Store a man was selling
incense. "It's very romantic," he said to me.
"I can't stand that stuff," I said. "Women love
it," he said. "It makes them want to make love."
"Not the women I know. That stuff would make
them leave me high and dry in a second," I said.
"You don't know the right women then. I could
introduce you to some. They all love this stuff,"
he said. This guy was really getting on my nerves.
"What are you, some kind of pimp? You stand
around the street selling this vile crap, and
then trying to sell women as well," I said.
"I didn't say anything about selling women. I
just said I could introduce you to some, some
real women who like to make love while smelling
this beautiful incense. That's no crime, I was
trying to be friendly and look where you take it,
calling me a pimp. If I weren't such a peace-
loving guy, I'd bust your ass," he said. Across
the street an old man on crutches fell down. "How
much is it?" I asked. People were helping the
old man up. His best days were over, that's for
sure. But he seemed determined to get somewhere.
"For you, they're a hundred dollars a stick," he
said. "Come on," I said, "I'm sorry I said what
I said. Let's forgive and forget. I'd really
like to buy some of that stuff," I said. "How
do you think it makes me feel selling this stuff,
huh? I'm a grown man and I'm selling incense on
the street. Is that a pretty picture? Do you

23

want to walk in my shoes?" he said. "Sorry, man," I said, and walked away. A flock of pigeons perched atop the First National Bank suddenly took flight, and I thought, this day is not over yet.

Suburban Bison

Joshua and I had decided to go bowling.
Neither of us had bowled in years, and we didn't
really like to bowl, so it made no sense. We
were driving down Route 9 when we spotted the
buffalo herd. They were grazing in the snow,
and something about their improbable heads made
me catch my breath. I pulled over to the side
of the road. "Why are they here?" Joshua asked.
"I guess it's some kind of cruel joke," I said.
"Well, it's not funny," he said. "They're way
too majestic. Buffalo are supposed to roam,
that's what the song says, not to be penned up
along some strip for tourists to see," he
said. "It beats bowling," I said. And so we
sat there for the next hour contemplating the
life of the postmodern buffalo, deconstructing
their owners, and never putting them back
together again.

In Search Of

Angela was sleeping all the time now, except for some quick meals and the odd bath. When we ate together she could barely talk. Finally I felt I had to say something. "Angela," I said, "I don't think this is good for you. You need exercise. And your mind . . . ." "I'm looking for something," she said, "something that will change our lives. And I'm getting closer. I think I may find it within a week. Please, trust me, be patient with me," she said. "What is it, Angela? What is it you are looking for?" I said. "I can't tell you. It would bring bad luck. You'll just have to trust me," she said, and went back to bed. During the following week we barely spoke. Then the next day she jumped out of bed, showered, dressed, and declared she was starving. She made herself an enormous meal and gulped it all down breathlessly. "Well, did you find it?" I asked. "Yeah, but it was a fake," she said. "What did you think it was going to be?" I asked. "I thought it was a finger of Saint John the Dwarf buried beneath the tulip tree out back, put there by marauding Berbers fifteen-hundred years ago. But it turns out it's just a plastic spoon," she said. I paused to let it all sink in. "Just think," I said, "a little piece of John the Dwarf in our backyard. And those marauding Berbers. I can see why you were excited."

Banking Rules

I was standing in line at the bank and
the fellow in front of me was humming. The
line was long and slow, and after a while
the humming began to irritate me. I said to
the fellow, "Excuse me, would you mind not
humming." And he said, "Was I humming?
I'm sorry, I didn't realize it." And he went
right on humming. I said, "Sir, you're
humming again." "Me, humming," he said.
"I don't think so." And then he went on
humming. I was about to blow my lid. Instead,
I went to find the manager. I said, "See
that man over there in the blue suit?" "Yes,"
he said, "what about him?" "He won't stop
humming," I said. "I've asked him politely
several times, but he won't stop." "There's
no crime in humming," he said. I went back
and took my place in line. I listened, but
there was nothing coming out of him. I said,
"Are you okay, pal?" He looked mildly peeved,
and gave me no reply. I felt myself shrinking.
The manager of the bank walked briskly up
to me and said, "Sir, are you aware of the
fact that you're shrinking?" I said I was.
And he said, "I'm afraid we don't allow that
kind of behavior in this bank. I have to ask
you to leave." The air was whistling out
of me, I was almost gone.

Heather's Men

A man stopped me on the street and said,
"Aren't you Victor Hewitt?" "That's me," I
said, "how did you know that?" "I'm a friend
of Julian's," he said. "I don't know any Julian,"
I said. "Julian's Heather's friend," he said.
"Heather Eston?" I asked. "Yeah, I think that's
her name," he said. "So why are you stopping me?"
I asked. "Heather showed me a picture of you," he
said. "Heather has a picture of me? I barely know
Heather Eston," I said. "Yeah, it was a funny
picture, too. You had some fruit on your head
or something," he said. "I never had any fruit
on my head," I said, "That's not something I would
do. I'm a serious guy, I don't put fruit on my
head." "Whatever," he said. "Heather said you
might know somebody who could help me do a job."
"What kind of job?" I said. "Just a job, you know.
A job," he said. "I know somebody who could
help you build a boat. I know somebody who
could help you build a house. I know somebody
who could help you build a mandolin," I said. "Very
funny," he said, "but I'm a serious man, too.
And I think you're the wrong Victor Hewitt,
or you're no Victor Hewitt at all." "I find
both thoughts very interesting, Bruno. I really
do," I said. "Hey, how'd you know my name is
Bruno?" he said, "I never told you my name."
"Heather told me," I said. "Wow," he said, looking
like he was trying to entertain a really big
thought, "and I thought I just made her up."

"You did, Bruno," I said, "and so did I. When two people like us work together, you see how powerful that can be. I'm definitely interested in working with you on that job. What are we going to do, free mice from a lab?" "You're beautiful!" he said, laughing, while nearly suffocating me with his fraternal bear hug.

The Search for Lost Lives

I was chasing this blue butterfly down
the road when a car came by and clipped me.
It was nothing serious, but it angered me and
I turned around and cursed the driver, who didn't
even slow down to see if I was hurt. Then I
returned my attention to the butterfly which
was nowhere to be seen. One of the Doubleday
girls came running up the street with her toy
poodle toward me. I stopped her and asked,
"Have you seen a blue butterfly around here?"
"It's down near that birch tree by Grandpa's,"
she said. "Thanks," I said, and walked briskly
toward the tree. It was fluttering from flower
to flower in Mr. Doubleday's extensive garden,
a celestial blueness to soothe the weary heart.
I didn't know what I was doing there. I certainly
didn't want to capture it. It was like
something I had known in another life, even if
it was only in a dream, I wanted to confirm it.
I was a blind beggar on the streets of Cordoba
when I first saw it, and now, again it was here.

The Animists

At the motel, the man said, "This is a
Christian motel. I've got to see your marriage
license." "Marriage license?" I said. "We don't
drive around with our marriage license. I don't
even know where it is, but it sure isn't in the
car." "Then you can't stay here. We don't allow
heathens," he said. "Heathens?" I said. "You're
calling us heathens?" "The world's full of them,"
he said. "Whether you're among them, I don't know.
But I don't take chances." "And how do we know
you're not some kind of child-molester or ax
murderer," Melissa said. I was proud of her.
"Show him your tits," I said. Melissa lifted up
her sweater and showed him her God-given natural
endowment. The old man gawked and stammered, "You . . .
you . . . appear to be Christian." "Nope," she said,
"the left one's an animist and the right one is
too private to even discuss religion, but my guess
is that she's an animist, too." "I like animists,"
he said, "I love animists. They're my favorite."
We turned and headed for the door. "Dirty old
man," I said. "You're right," he said. "I am
a dirty old Christian man. I didn't know that.
Thank you and come back any time."

The Healing Ground

Mimi was going to take me to her special
place, some kind of sacred healing ground, though
she never said whose. For over a year walking had
caused me great pain, and none of the doctors I
had seen gave me any help. I viewed Mimi's invitation
as an excuse for an outing. I know the country
around here pretty well, but when Mimi started
turning down one twisting dirt road after another
at some point I knew I was lost. Mimi's a reliable
person, nothing of the fruitcake in her. When she
finally stopped, the first thing I noticed was a
hole in the side of the hill surrounded by boulders.
"What's that?" I said. "An Irish monk lived in there
some time in the sixteenth century," she said.
"The Indians took care of him. They thought he
was a holy man." "Do I have to crawl in there?"
I asked. "Oh no, nothing like that," she said.
"They say he lived in that hole for thirty years,
praying all the time." "I wonder what happened
to him. Did the Church make him a saint?" I said.
"Something ate him, a bear or a mountain lion. The
Indians thought it was a mountain lion," she said.
"Mimi," I said, "did you bring me all the way out
here just to tell me this story, not that it isn't
a great story, 'cause it is, but I'd also love to
see this 'healing ground,' is that possible?"
"It's right over there in that clearing. Come
on, I'll show you," she said. We had to push our
way through the brush and climb over some fallen
trees. It wasn't that easy for me to get there,

32

but we got there, and I looked around, but could
see nothing special about the place. I mentioned
that to Mimi. "Except for that fairy ring of
mushrooms. That's pretty cute," I said. "You have
to stand in there and pray for the soul of the Irish
monk for ten minutes. That's all," she said. There's
a new fruitcake status in store for you, Mimi, I
thought. "If that's what it takes," I said, "I'll
do it." I proceeded to stand in the circle of
mushrooms with my eyes closed and, sure enough,
I prayed for the soul of the little Irish monk.
He would have had to be little, because the hole
wasn't all that big. I thought of his rosary and
his Bible, and the long winters of terrible cold
and snow. And his great peace when he met the lion.

A Sound Like Distant Thunder

I had fallen asleep on the couch with the
TV on. Every now and then I would open an eye
and see someone get stabbed or eaten by a monster.
Once, a beautiful woman was taking off her blouse.
And then the phone rang. I couldn't tell if it
was a TV phone or my own. I sat up, half-asleep,
and reached for the phone. "Howie," a woman's
voice said, "Is that you? You sound like you were
asleep." "I was," I said. I wasn't Howie, but
I was in the mood to talk to this woman. "Howie,
I miss you. I wish I were in bed with you right
now," she said. "I miss you, too. I wish you
were here with me right now," I said. I hated
not knowing her name, and I didn't know if I could
call her "honey" or "sweetie" or any other endear-
ment. "Why don't you come over right now," I
said. "Oh you know I'm in Australia. And my
work here won't be done for another month. It's
just hell being away from you this long," she said.
"I love you," I said, and I think I meant it.
"You mean the world to me, Howie. I couldn't get
through this without knowing you love me. I think
of you all the time. I look at your picture
every chance I get. It's what gives me strength,
that and our brief phone calls. Now go back to
sleep and dream of me, dream of me kissing you
and holding you. I have to go now. I love you,
Howie," she said and hung up. And though my state
may be described as a gladdened stupor, I felt
like a Howie, I really did, and I believed in my

heart that the nameless, faceless one indentured in Australia really loved me, and that my great love for her gave her strength. I cozied up on the couch and fell into a sweet sleep. But then I heard a lion roar, and I feared for both of our lives. "Howie!" she cried. "Save me!" But I couldn't. I was busy elsewhere, tying my shoe.

James Tate's *Selected Poems* was published in 1991, for which he received the Pulitzer Prize and the William Carlos Williams Award. His volume of poems, *Worshipful Company of Fletchers*, published in 1994, was awarded the National Book Award. In 1995, the Academy of American Poets presented him with the Tanning Prize. *Shroud of the Gnome* was published by Ecco Press in 1997. His newest volume of poems, *Memoir of the Hawk*, is also available from Ecco Press. Tate teaches at the University of Massachusetts.